10

Swe
&
Cand

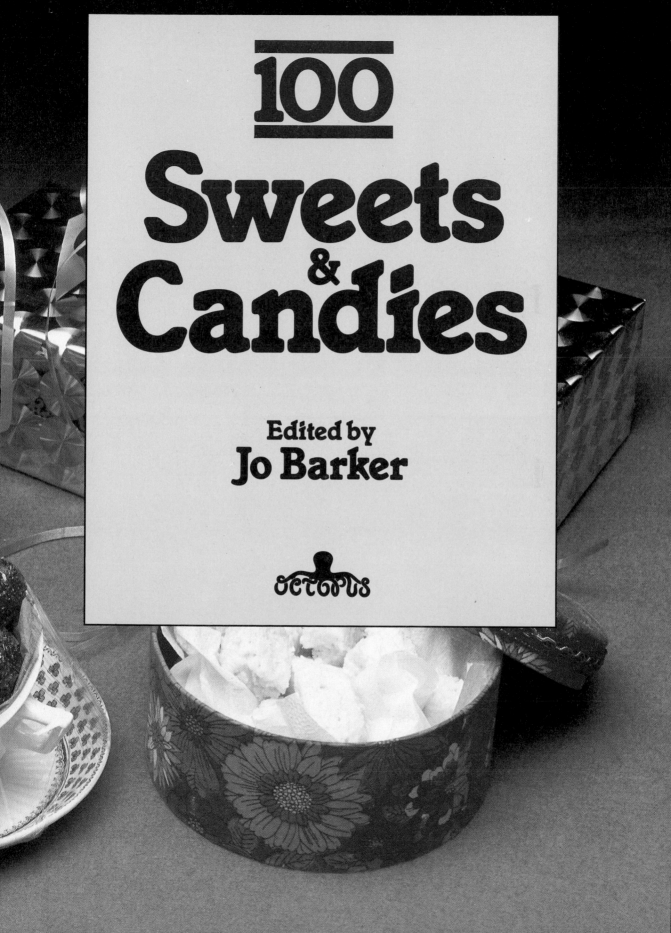

100
Sweets & Candies

Edited by
Jo Barker

octopus

Contents

NOTES
Standard spoon measurements are used in all recipes
1 tablespoon = one 15 ml spoon
1 teaspoon = one 5 ml spoon
All spoon measures are level.

For all recipes, quantities are given in metric, imperial and American measures. Follow one set of measures only, because they are not interchangeable.
Ovens should always be preheated to the specified temperature.

First published 1983 by
Octopus Books Limited
59 Grosvenor Street, London W1

© 1983 Octopus Books Limited

ISBN 0 7064 1951 0

Produced by Mandarin Publishers Ltd
22a Westlands Rd
Quarry Bay, Hong Kong

Printed in Hong Kong

Frontispiece: a selection of homemade sweets and candies (Photograph: Kraft Foods)